I AM
PROUD OF ME
AF439114

I AM
GETTING SMARTER
DAILY

I AM
AN ACHIEVER

MY SPIRIT
IS CONFIDENT

I TRUST
MY ABILITIES

I AM LIVING WITH A PURPOSE

I AM

PASSIONATE

ABOUT SUCCESS

I WILL CREATE BETTER HABITS

I DON'T
NEED APPROVAL
FROM OTHERS

I BELIEVE
IN MY IDEAS

I AM ENERGIZED AND READY TO SUCCEED

I AM
MOTIVATED TO
ACCOMPLISH MY
GOALS

I DON'T
BREAK UNDER
PRESSURE

I AM
CREATIVE
AND
PERSISTENT

I AM
FOCUSED
ON MY GOALS

I KNOW MY
WORTH

I AM
COMFORTABLE
WITH ABUNDANCE

I PUSH MYSELF
TO FOLLOW
MY DREAMS

I ATTRACT
HAPPINES

I MAKE GREAT

CONTRIBUTIONS

I CAN
LET GO
OF NEGATIVE
THOUGHTS

I ATTRACT

GOOD

CIRCUMSTANCES

I WILL
CONQUER ALL
OBSTACLES

I WILL
MAKE WISE
DECISIONS

I TRUST
MY JOURNEY